AFTER HIS OWN HEART

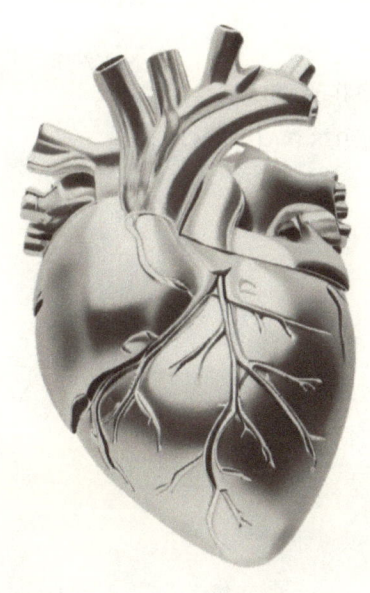

After His Own Heart

Copyright © 2025 by Francesca Villani (equally identified by author name F. C. Villani).

All rights reserved under Copyright Act 1968. Published in Australia. Printed domestically and internationally.

No part of this book may be used or reproduced without written permission by the author, except in the case of reviews, critical articles, or promotion.

All Scriptures used in this book have been taken from the NASB1995 Bible and the NKJV Bible.

Editing by: Abigayle Claire (Glory Writers)

Ebook ISBN: 978-0-6457054-4-7

Paperback ISBN: 978-0-6457054-5-4

Table of Contents

Introduction 11
How To Read This Book............................13

Part I

David: A Man of Understanding....................17
David: A Man of Spiritual Warfare….....………21

Part II

Psalm 1…..31
Psalm 2…..33
Psalm 3…..36
Psalm 4…..41
Psalm 5…..43
Psalm 6…..46
Psalm 7…..51
Psalm 8…..54
Psalm 9…..56
Psalm 10…...63
Psalm 11…...67
Psalm 12…...69

Psalm 13..73
Psalm 14..75
Psalm 15..77
Psalm 16..81
Psalm 17..84
Psalm 18..87
Psalm 19..95
Psalm 20..98
Psalm 21..101
Psalm 22..105
Psalm 23..109
Psalm 24..111
Psalm 25..115
Psalm 26..119
Psalm 27..122
Psalm 28..129
Psalm 29..131
Psalm 30..133

About The Author
Also By F C Villani

Disclaimer

Please note that while David wrote most of the Psalms of the Bible, not all of them are accounted for by him. Nevertheless, as written in 2 Timothy 3:16-17, "All Scripture is inspired by God and profitable for teaching, for reproof, for correction, for training in righteousness; so that the man of God may be adequate, equipped for every good work."

Therefore, although David was named as a man after God's own heart, we know that God's word is His own, and even the Psalms not attributed to David were written by the inspiration of God's own Spirit. As a result, they all carry the heart of God.

Also, you may find portions of the following prayers as literal quotes from their corresponding Psalm. This was done intentionally, as while writing them I could not ignore the conviction in my spirit to keep them as they were. Why try to rewrite a prayer that is already written so perfectly in the Scriptures?

To He who delights in a righteous heart.

"One thing I have desired of the Lord, that I will seek: that I may dwell in the house of the Lord all the days of my life, to behold the beauty of the Lord, and to inquire in His temple."

-

Psalm 27:4

Introduction

Lately it has been my desire to be like King David—to have a heart after God's own. I want to be a person of integrity. A person who when given the opportunity to slaughter my enemy chooses instead to honour the Lord. A person who inquires of the Lord frequently and without partiality. A person who is not given to fear in the presence of a giant foe but stands firm on His faith. A person who knows their Lord and has such an intimate relationship with Him that I am able to trust Him and His character with all confidence and persuasion.

I had just woken up from my sleep when an idea popped into my head as if of its own accord: to write prayers based on the Psalms. It nagged at me until I wrote it down in my notes. That day, I got started on this book. I had gone into this with a very practical motive, figuring that the best way to learn what separated David would be to read his writings, which would make me understand his heart, so I could then pray for what I found there to mould my own heart. What I didn't expect was for my heart to be transformed in the midst of my studies. What I didn't anticipate was to be brought to tears, psalm after psalm. My heart was exposed simultaneously in my pursuit to expose David's. I began to see the Lord through the eyes of a man whose heart desired the Lord's face more than anything else. I pray this would be your experience as you pray these prayers.

If it is your desire to be intimate with our Father, to worship Him in spirit and in truth, to be moulded and refined for His glory, then I ask that you pray your own personal prayer before proceeding further. Pray that the Lord would reveal Himself to you, that He would break your heart for what breaks His, that He would speak to you and minister to you through these prayers, and pray that He would give you a heart after His own.

With love,

Francesca Villani

How To Read This Book

First and foremost, do a little self-evaluation and discern for yourself the best way you can read this book to get the most out of it. Go to your quiet and private place, the place and state that only you and the Lord share. Be intentional. And be mindful that the enemy wants to steal, kill, and destroy your prayer time. So try to recognise distractions and be honest with yourself, because sometimes we can aid the enemy here in his quest to hinder us by giving in to excuses, to doubts, to other priorities and obligations. But the fact that Jesus committed Himself to prayer, the fact that David was in constant communication with the Lord and that communication often led to David being blessed, being protected, and being honoured by the Lord, tells me one thing: I can't afford to demote prayer to the bottom of my list of things to do. If I want to hear Him, if I want to recognise Him, if I want to behold His glory and become like Him, with a heart after His own, I need to elevate His place on my list to first, and I need to talk to Him.

Verses to meditate on and pray into if you are struggling with this:

Matthew 6:33; Colossians 3:23; 1 Corinthians 10:31; Romans 12:1; Proverbs 16:3; Proverbs 4:26

P.S. it is a common struggle among the Lord's people (myself included!) so don't feel disheartened, but now you are met with a question: what are you going to do about it?

F. C. Villani

Part I

F. C. Villani

David: A Man of Understanding

One thing that was made very clear to me while reading through the Psalms is that David was a man of deep understanding. A heart of understanding is actually what King David's son Solomon requests from the Lord in 1 Kings 3. It's my belief that Solomon perceived the great understanding in his father David and was able to recognise that this is what led to David being a king who walked in truth, righteousness, and uprightness, and what ignited the kindness and favour of the Lord to pour out onto him and his generations.

As you read the Psalms attributed to David, you begin to see that David knew the character of God. He understood God. And this understanding led to David's ability to depend and rely on God, to feel safe with Him, to trust in Him, to praise Him, to encourage others to seek Him, to act with the motivation of giving God glory, to walk in integrity, to inquire of the Lord, to be honest with Him, to have an intolerance to evil and wickedness, to be humble, and to be in awe of God.

It causes me to ask myself, do I know God in this way? Do I understand God as David did? Why even stop there? Why not seek to understand the Father as Jesus did? When I consider the life of David and the time Jesus spent on earth before returning to

His throne, I see what it was that led to their understanding of the Father: presence.

David acknowledged the connection between understanding God and the presence of God in the revelation of Psalm 14:2:

> *"The Lord looks down from heaven upon the children of men, To see if there are any who understand, who seek God."*

What this looks like to me is that first I must seek God. When I seek Him, His Word promises that I will find Him — that as I draw closer to Him, He will draw closer to me. When we have drawn to one another, we are now abiding in each other's presence. The good Lord bundles me up in His presence where I am able to see Him rightly, where I'm able to learn about Him, where I am able to find rest. And if I dwell in that presence long enough, intentional enough, I will reach greater understanding.

It starts with His presence, it lasts in His presence, it ends in His presence. I am preserved in His presence. I am given the fullness of His joy in His presence. I am directed and guided in His presence. I am close enough that I can hear what He desires to whisper to me. I am so near that I am able to remain prostrate before Him. I am brought to my knees before His throne and am only able to lift my face before Him because I understand He has given me a seat in heavenly places, to sit with Him, at His table, even though my humanity would have me begging at His doorstep in vain. This holy God adopted me into the inheritance of all He has, because He loves me and chose me before I ever considered Him. This beautiful God, who fathers me like I am His precious child, who loves me as if my shortcomings, my tantrums, my faults, my mistakes, don't have a single impact on His unconditional love for me.

But I can only gain this level of understanding in His presence. In His Word. I must be still, desist in all I am doing, that I may *know* God. That I may *learn*.

I pray you would continue through this book and pray these prayers with a hunger to understand your Father and know Him deeply, and I pray these prayers would cause your heart to be broken for what breaks His, to be moulded by His hands, to be softened, and above all, to be transformed into a heart that replicates the Father's heart and is manifested through every aspect of your life.

F. C. Villani

David: A Man of Spiritual Warfare

What is our warfare strategy?

Maybe I should first ask this: *where is the battlefield?* You can't strategise without the location of battle, because your strategy will always be dependent on where your fight takes place. Through Jesus Christ our spirit is renewed, and yet while our spirit has been saved from death, our flesh can still be used as a vessel for evil. Why? Because our flesh is at war with our spirit. It still wills to do what the spirit does not. You might think then that our flesh is the battlefield. Not necessarily, because what controls the flesh? The mind. This is why we are instructed in Romans 12:2 to *"not be conformed to this world by being transformed by the renewing of our mind."*

Scientifically, the brain is able to do this through a process known as neuroplasticity, in which the brain is able to change and grow by creating neural pathways which are strengthened over use. These neural pathways are birthed out of new behaviour. Repeatedly performing the new behaviour causes the neural pathways that zap and send messages around the brain to work more effectively, and actually causes other neural pathways to, in a sense, die, from lack of use. It's similar to the way denying our flesh strengthens our inner man, strengthens our spirit.

Your default reactions and responses can be changed, but it takes effort on our part to create the new neural pathways.

If I was the enemy, I would do everything I could to infiltrate a person's mind. This is why what we fill our mind with is so important and so conducive to the way we live our lives. Just like if I were to fill my body with non-nutritious trash that causes my body to function improperly, filling my mind with lies and worldly desires causes my brain to work in a way it shouldn't if I want to live the abundant life Jesus sacrificed Himself for.

While I cannot pretend to know if David knew the science behind what he was doing when it came to spiritual warfare, I can say boldly that I constantly find passages in the Psalms where David fought the enemy on the battlefield of his mind, and won.

What I'm about to say is not from biblical revelation, but only my opinion: if the enemy fought David as hard as he did to inhibit the work of God, fought a man who did not have the Holy Spirit living inside of him, then how much more is the enemy going to come after those who have accepted Jesus Christ as Saviour and have been filled with the Helper, the Holy Spirit, who are the vessels for God's grace and will to overcome the earth?

Paul says in 2 Corinthians 10:3-6:

> "For though we walk in the flesh, we do not war according to the flesh, for the weapons of our warfare are not of the flesh, but divinely powerful for the destruction of fortresses. We are destroying speculations and every lofty thing raised up against the knowledge of God, and we are taking every thought captive to the obedience of Christ, and we are ready to punish all disobedience, whenever your obedience is complete."

Taking every thought captive to the obedience of Christ means that every single thought I have must obey Jesus. What I think about must align with the word and promises of God.

Read how David does this in Psalm 8:4-5:

> "What is man that You take thought of him, And the son of man that You care for him? Yet You have made him a little lower than God, And You crown him with glory and majesty!"

David is questioning the Lord, asking Him *'who am I that You are mindful of me?'* But watch this: David's wonder of why God would be mindful of him was not evidence that God could not be mindful of him. I believe David knew this very thing: my questioning of a thing is not my evidence of a thing.

James 3:17 says this,

> "But the wisdom of above is first pure, peace-loving, gentle, willing to yield, full of mercy and good fruits, impartial, free of hypocrisy."

And it is here we find *Strategy #1:* if the thought in my mind does not align with the description of God's wisdom given to me in James 3:17, I will test the thought until it is.

Notice that a part of that description is that the wisdom of above is 'free of hypocrisy'. Therefore, if the thought you have contradicts the word of God, it is not God's wisdom.

Those verses in Psalm 8 were prompted by David considering the works of God, the heavens, the moon and the stars. He is in awe at the beauty and mass of God's creation, and the dominion God has given man over His creation. How quickly could this moment of wonder and reverence be twisted by the enemy for David's ruin? Imagine if David had ceased his meditations on questioning his worth before God. Can you imagine the rabbit hole he would have fallen through? Can you imagine the imposter syndrome? The self-doubt? The feelings of inadequacy? The shame?

But instead David continues in Psalm 8 to declare the goodness of God, giving glory to God, and reminding himself of God's will for man. I wonder, is this the blueprint we should be using to successfully take our minds captive?

Maybe where we go wrong is not in us getting the thought, but in how we finish the thought.

When a thought enters your mind, are you letting it sit and stew, or are you finishing the thought with the truth and wisdom and love of God?

Seen all throughout his writings is David's **Strategy #2:** instruct the soul and the heart based on your knowledge of God and not on your circumstance.

In Psalm 13, David starts off in desperation asking God a series of 'how long?' questions. We can probably relate to that. How long, God? How long will this go on? How long must I endure? How long must I suffer? How long until I get what You said I'd get? However, David ends Psalm 13 in a completely different light. He goes from pleading to God for an answer, to telling the Lord *"my heart shall rejoice in Your salvation"*, and then telling himself *"I will sing to the Lord, because He has dealt bountifully with me"*.

What I take from this is that despite his situation, and despite not getting the help he was hoping to have gotten by then, David was able to reflect on what he knew of God and what God had already done for him.

Psalm 22 is incredible to bear witness to. It is the Scripture that Jesus quotes on the cross, and it is powerful. Over half of this Psalm, David is describing to God the way he is suffering. It is a suffering that mirrors the suffering of Jesus in many ways, i.e. the nailing of hands and feet, the casting of lots for his garments. In it David tells God *"I cry by day, but You do not answer; and by night, but I have no rest."* Immediately, he says *"yet You are holy"*, and honours the Lord by declaring the way He has delivered His people. And then, incredibly, after going into heart-breaking detail of his suffering, David has this back and forth monologue where he goes from declaring that he will praise God, to encouraging all the people of Israel to stand in awe of God, how God hears the afflicted and helps them, to going back to God and declaring that "all the families of the nation with worship before You!"

How does a person go from a desperate cry for help to not only praising God, but glorifying His name to others? By having a knowledge of God that surpasses the logic and worldly perception of your situation and understanding.

However, there are instances of warfare where knowledge on its own just isn't enough. We have to use it. We have to exercise the authority and dominion and grace bestowed on us by Father God through Jesus Christ, and a part of that means to make our flesh subject to our renewed minds.

Lastly, *Strategy #3:* committing to self-control and maturity. In Psalm 131:2, David says this,

> "Surely I have composed and quieted my soul; like a weaned child rests against his mother, my soul is like a weaned child within me."

One of the prominent meanings of the Hebrew word 'damam', which is used in this verse for 'quieted', is *silence*. David got his soul under the control of himself, and silenced it. He then describes his soul as a *'weaned child'*. The process of weaning is to accustom a baby who has only ever had milk from its mother's breast to different, solid foods. As David has accustomed himself to what is pleasing to God, so should we. And so can we, through the Holy Spirit.

As Paul says in 1 Corinthians 13:11,

> "When I was a child, I used to speak like a child, think like a child, reason like a child; when I became a man, I did away with childish things."

To triumph in spiritual warfare, we must put away childish things. We must discard them. It takes an action on our part to become as a weaned child, off the diet of spiritual milk, and nourished by the solid foods of the Spirit.

Part II

F. C. Villani

PSALM 1

Scripture:

How blessed is the man who does not walk in the counsel of the wicked, Nor stand in the path of sinners, Nor sit in the seat of scoffers! But his delight is in the law of the Lord, And in His law he meditates day and night. He will be like a tree firmly planted by streams of water, Which yields its fruit in its season And its leaf does not wither; And in whatever he does, he prospers. The wicked are not so, But they are like chaff which the wind drives away. Therefore the wicked will not stand in the judgment, Nor sinners in the assembly of the righteous. For the Lord knows the way of the righteous, But the way of the wicked will perish.

Prayer:

Father God in heaven,

Make me a person who walks only in godly counsel, and not someone who walks an ungodly, unrighteous path. Make me a person who delights in You, Lord, and in all the things that please You. Make me a person who desires to meditate on Your word day and night, that I may be transformed by it, and so my heart and mind may remain on the things of the kingdom, and not on myself or worldly things. Make me a person who is like a tree planted by rivers of water, that brings forth fruit in its season, whose leaf also does not wither, that whatever I do may prosper, Lord, for Your glory. Lead me, Father, and purify my heart that I may not become like the ungodly, who are like the chaff which the wind drives away. You know the way of the righteous, Lord, and You are the Good Shepherd who leads us on the path of righteousness, and so lead me, Father God, that I may not perish, but be blessed with You.

In Jesus' name I pray, amen.

PSALM 2

Scripture

Why are the nations in an uproar And the peoples devising a vain thing? The kings of the earth take their stand And the rulers take counsel together Against the Lord and against His Anointed, saying, "Let us tear their fetters apart And cast away their cords from us!" He who sits in the heavens laughs, The Lord scoffs at them. Then He will speak to them in His anger And terrify them in His fury, saying, "But as for Me, I have installed My King Upon Zion, My holy mountain." "I will surely tell of the decree of the Lord: He said to Me, 'You are My Son, Today I have begotten You. Ask of Me, and I will surely give the nations as Your inheritance, And the very ends of the earth as Your possession. You shall break them with a rod of iron, You shall shatter them like earthenware.'" Now therefore, O kings, show discernment; Take warning, O judges of the earth. Worship the Lord with reverence And rejoice with trembling. Do homage to the Son, that He not become angry, and you perish in the way, For His wrath may soon be kindled. How blessed are all who take refuge in Him!

F. C. Villani

Prayer

Father God in heaven,

Although there are people in this world who plot evil in their hearts and minds in vain, and although anger sweeps the nations, and although the authorities of this world establish themselves in themselves and not in You, and take each other's counsel over Yours, and try to plot against You and Your anointed people, they shall not prevail. Your power is greater than these, Lord God, so much so that You laugh in heaven. Purify my heart, Lord, that I may never cause You such displeasure, and shall never elevate myself above You. I thank You that I can come boldly to Your throne of grace and ask anything of You. I thank You that You protect me against my enemies, and against those who plot against You, and I thank You that You are mightier than they, and their ways shall not stand. Make me wise, Father God, that I may heed Your instruction, and strengthen my fear for You, Father, that wisdom may also be strengthened in me, and I may give glory to You. Convict the rulers of this world, and all those who think they are wise in their own eyes, and reveal to them Your power, Your authority, and Your truth. Turn their hearts of stone to hearts of flesh, Lord, and give them eyes to see and ears to hear, that they may come to You with a contrite spirit and receive You, Jesus, into their hearts. Help us to put all of our trust in You, Lord, that we may be blessed.

In Jesus' name I pray, amen.

PSALM 3

Scripture

O Lord, how my adversaries have increased! Many are rising up against me. Many are saying of my soul, "There is no deliverance for him in God." Selah. But You, O Lord, are a shield about me, My glory, and the One who lifts my head. I was crying to the Lord with my voice, And He answered me from His holy mountain. Selah. I lay down and slept; I awoke, for the Lord sustains me. I will not be afraid of ten thousands of people Who have set themselves against me round about. Arise, O Lord; save me, O my God! For You have smitten all my enemies on the cheek; You have shattered the teeth of the wicked. Salvation belongs to the Lord; Your blessing be upon Your people! Selah.

Prayer

Father God,

I am surrounded by enemies. It seems that those who trouble me have doubled, and many rise up against me, whether that be physically in person or in the spirit. And although some of them might doubt You are here to help me, I know, O Lord, You are a shield for me against all of them. You are the One who lifts up my head when I am downcast, when my focus falls off the things of above, and I have forgotten who I am and what You have spoken. When I have cried to You, Father, You have heard me. You have heard me! You give me rest, so much so that I can lay down and sleep amidst my enemies and awake without harm, for You, Lord God, my Father, have sustained me and keep sustaining me. I will not be afraid of anyone who has set themselves against me, for You are the Lord of hosts, and Your power is greater than theirs. I am Yours, and I am blessed because You have blessed me. Save me from their plans, save me from their wickedness, save me from their selfish ambition and motives, Father. Give me eyes and ears to discern my enemies, Father, and use me so that they may see my good works and glorify You despite their flesh.

In Jesus' name I pray, amen.

Refine me Potter. I am Your clay, made for Your glory.

The Potter & the clay

The Lord is an artist. He is the giver of the gift of craftsmanship, and He is an expert with His hands. And like a potter, the Lord works intimately with His clay, holding it up with His hands, sinking His fingers into the areas of refinement, creating grooves and crevices for pruning and perfecting. He lays the foundation, that the clay may be stable on its feet. He adds to it, only what the clay can manage, and even when the clay cannot bear the weight, His hands are there, wrapped around the clay, preserving it, that it may lean on the Potter, and remain upright. What must be acknowledged is that the Potter does not stop until His work is done. The Potter is there as a support, like the ever-present hand of a parent to a baby taking its first steps. But do not misunderstand the Potter, for the Potter will also press firmly and squeeze. Why do you despise His pressure? For how can a clay vessel be crafted into the shape of its purpose if pressure is not applied to it? Was a vase born a vase? Or did it begin as a lump of the earth, where it was then given to the Potter and transformed? You are not a vase, for a vase is the finished work. You are the lump, subject to the Potter. Therefore be as soft clay, that is, mouldable, and not as hard rock, which cannot be penetrated. For a rock cannot be transformed into anything, but remains as a rock, and thus, useless for the Lord's will.

PSALM 4

Scripture

Answer me when I call, O God of my righteousness! You have relieved me in my distress; Be gracious to me and hear my prayer. O sons of men, how long will my honor become a reproach? How long will you love what is worthless and aim at deception? Selah. But know that the Lord has set apart the godly man for Himself; The Lord hears when I call to Him. Tremble, and do not sin; Meditate in your heart upon your bed, and be still. Selah. Offer the sacrifices of righteousness, And trust in the Lord. Many are saying, "Who will show us any good?" Lift up the light of Your countenance upon us, O Lord! You have put gladness in my heart, More than when their grain and new wine abound. In peace I will both lie down and sleep, For You alone, O Lord, make me to dwell in safety.

Prayer

Father God in heaven,

Hear me when I call, O God of my righteousness! Relieve me in my distress. Incline Your ear to me and hear my prayer. Have grace and favour upon me, Father God. May I never be a vessel for the enemy to put others to shame, or a lover of worthless things, or a seeker of what is false in Your eyes. Set me apart for You, Lord. Make me a person that when I am angry I do not sin. Put a burden and urgency on my heart, Father God, to meditate within my heart on my bed, and to be still. Have Your reward in me, Lord God. Teach me what it means to deny myself and offer the sacrifices of righteousness to You, Lord, and to put my whole trust in You. If I have ever questioned in my heart 'who will show me any good?' Lord, I pray You would lift up the light of Your countenance upon me. I thank You that Your presence brings with it the fullness of Your joy. Make gladness to dwell in my heart, Lord, more than it has in any season before. I will both lie down in peace, and sleep; for You alone, O Lord, make me dwell in safety. Thank You.

In Jesus' name I pray, amen.

PSALM 5

Scripture

Give ear to my words, O Lord, Consider my groaning. Heed the sound of my cry for help, my King and my God, For to You I pray. In the morning, O Lord, You will hear my voice; In the morning I will order my prayer to You and eagerly watch. For You are not a God who takes pleasure in wickedness; No evil dwells with You. The boastful shall not stand before Your eyes; You hate all who do iniquity. You destroy those who speak falsehood; The Lord abhors the man of bloodshed and deceit. But as for me, by Your abundant lovingkindness I will enter Your house, At Your holy temple I will bow in reverence for You. O Lord, lead me in Your righteousness because of my foes; Make Your way straight before me. There is nothing reliable in what they say; Their inward part is destruction itself. Their throat is an open grave; They flatter with their tongue. Hold them guilty, O God; By their own devices let them fall! In the multitude of their transgressions thrust them out, For they are rebellious against You. But let all who take refuge in You be glad, Let them ever sing for joy; And may You shelter them, That those who love Your name may exult in You. For it is You

> who blesses the righteous man, O Lord, You surround him with favor as with a shield.

Prayer

Holy Father God,

Give ear to my words, and consider the meditations of my heart. Give heed to the voice of my cry, My King and my God, for to You alone I will pray. Give me a hunger and desire to give You my voice in the mornings, O Lord, so You shall hear it. I will direct my voice to You in the mornings, and I will look up, for You are worthy of my time and my adoration and devotion. Make it that my eyes are fixed upon You from the moment I wake, Lord God. For You are not a God who takes pleasure in wickedness, nor can evil dwell with You. Make me so that evil does not dwell within me either, Lord, that nothing in my heart or mind or flesh may separate me from You and all the things found in You. I repent if I have been boastful and have been working in iniquity, whether I am aware of it or not. Purify me of this, that I may be pleasing in Your sight, Lord. May no false word leave my lips, and may I be a person who only speaks life. Cleanse me, Lord, if there is any deceit in me, and show me what to do when I am faced with deceit in another. I thank You, Lord, that I can come boldly to Your throne of grace, in the multitude of Your mercy.

Bless Your Holy Name. Give me pure and steadfast fear of the Lord, that I may worship You purely, in spirit and in truth. Lead me, O Lord, in Your righteousness and make Your way straight before my face. Let me not be led or deceived by the flattery of others, or their faithlessness, or the destruction in those around me. To those people, convict their hearts and cause them to turn from their ways, and turn to You in pure repentance. Strengthen my faith in Your word, Lord, that I may shout for joy, believing You defend me, and strengthen my devotion to You, that my love for Your Name would make me joyful in You. Thank You for being a shield around me, Lord, and for having favour upon me. Bless Your Holy Name.

In Jesus' name I pray, amen.

PSALM 6

Scripture

O Lord, do not rebuke me in Your anger, Nor chasten me in Your wrath. Be gracious to me, O Lord, for I am pining away; Heal me, O Lord, for my bones are dismayed. And my soul is greatly dismayed; But You, O Lord—how long? Return, O Lord, rescue my soul; Save me because of Your lovingkindness. For there is no mention of You in death; In Sheol who will give You thanks? I am weary with my sighing; Every night I make my bed swim, I dissolve my couch with my tears. My eye has wasted away with grief; It has become old because of all my adversaries. Depart from me, all you who do iniquity, For the Lord has heard the voice of my weeping. The Lord has heard my supplication, The Lord receives my prayer. All my enemies will be ashamed and greatly dismayed; They shall turn back, they will suddenly be ashamed.

Prayer

Father God,

I thank You for the cross, and that because of it I can come boldly to Your throne of grace. I come to You with a contrite heart. If my heart is not repentant, make it so. You know me, and You search my heart, and if it is not repentant before You, Father, convict me. Increase my reverent fear for You, Father, for You are worthy of my reasonable service. I thank You that Your strength is made perfect in my weakness. Redeem me, Father God. My heart aches. My spirit is troubled. I am aware of myself in this moment. Free me from all those who work in iniquity, Father God, and who try to lead me into iniquity. Deliver me from my enemies. Deliver me from myself, and have Your reward in me. Thank You for receiving me, Father.

In Jesus' name I pray, amen.

Order me, Commander. I am Your soldier, faithful to the end of my service.

The Commander & the soldier

The Lord is the Lord of hosts. All things are subject to Him. But you He has called to fight the good fight. You are His soldier. You were given the weapons of warfare. You were commanded to put on the whole armour of God, that you may be able to withstand the wiles of the enemy. Why do you behave as if it were another person, and not you, called to this? Why do you treat the weapons of warfare as if they are not yours to take hold of? Can a butcher slice the cow without a butcher's knife? Or can a farmer plant with no seeds? Why then do you go about your day, knowing very well the enemy of this world, without your Sword? Without girding yourself? Are you that proud that you don't think the word of God applies to you? But I say to you, take up your shield of faith, your helmet of salvation, your breastplate of righteousness, your sword of the Spirit which is the word of God, your belt of truth, with the gospel of peace at your feet always. Present yourself to the Commander equipped and armed, as a soldier who awaits instruction before his army general. Be used for His glory, for His kingdom, showing reverence to the Lord by being obedient.

PSALM 7

Scripture

O Lord my God, in You I have taken refuge; Save me from all those who pursue me, and deliver me, Or he will tear my soul like a lion, Dragging me away, while there is none to deliver. O Lord my God, if I have done this, If there is injustice in my hands, If I have rewarded evil to my friend, Or have plundered him who without cause was my adversary, Let the enemy pursue my soul and overtake it; And let him trample my life down to the ground And lay my glory in the dust. Selah. Arise, O Lord, in Your anger; Lift up Yourself against the rage of my adversaries, And arouse Yourself for me; You have appointed judgment. Let the assembly of the peoples encompass You, And over them return on high. The Lord judges the peoples; Vindicate me, O Lord, according to my righteousness and my integrity that is in me. O let the evil of the wicked come to an end, but establish the righteous; For the righteous God tries the hearts and minds. My shield is with God, Who saves the upright in heart. God is a righteous judge, And a God who has indignation every day. If a man does not repent, He will sharpen His sword; He has bent His bow and made it ready. He has also prepared for Himself deadly weapons; He makes His arrows fiery shafts. Behold, he travails with wickedness, And he conceives mischief and brings forth falsehood. He has dug a pit and hollowed it out, And has fallen into the hole which he made. His mischief will return upon his own head, And his violence will descend upon his own pate. I will give thanks to the Lord according to His righteousness And will sing praise to the name of the Lord Most High.

Prayer

O Lord my God, in You I put my trust. Save me from all those who persecute me and deliver me, lest they tear me like a lion, rending me in pieces, while there is none to deliver. O Lord my God, if I have done this myself, if there is iniquity in my hands, if I have repaid evil to him who was at peace with me, or have plundered my enemy without cause, convict my heart. Give me Your wisdom, Your understanding, Your knowledge, and Your discernment. Do not allow me to tolerate myself if I have done this, Lord, but give me eyes to see and ears to hear. Show me where I have gone wrong and why. Humble me and restore me. Restore forgiveness if I lack it, or if I have provoked unforgiveness in another. You are my Defender, Lord. In Your righteous anger, You protect me, and You go before me. Vengeance is Yours; do not let me steal it from You. Have Your way in my enemies, Father God, and have Your way in me. You are my righteous Judge, so judge my conduct, if it is righteous, and make me live in righteousness and integrity. Establish the just in my life, Father, but if wickedness surrounds me, put an end to it. Test my heart and mind, that my faith may be strengthened, my heart purified, and my mind renewed. I praise You again, Lord, for You are my Defender, and You save the upright in heart. You are a just Judge, and Your anger is aroused by wickedness. Deliver those in my life who have turned away from You, Lord, and if I can be used as a vessel to draw them closer to You, then let it be so Father. Speak through me. Use me according to Your perfect will. Deliver the wicked hearts around me so they cease to bring forth iniquity, so they do not conceive trouble or falsehood. Deliver those who stir trouble, and the violent, that they may bear testimony of Your grace and goodness, instead of reaping the harvest of wicked seeds. You are worthy of my praise, Lord Most High. Be glorified. Be magnified, Lord of truth and righteousness.

In Jesus' name I pray, amen.

PSALM 8

Scripture

O Lord, our Lord, How majestic is Your name in all the earth, Who have displayed Your splendor above the heavens! From the mouth of infants and nursing babes You have established strength Because of Your adversaries, To make the enemy and the revengeful cease. When I consider Your heavens, the work of Your fingers, The moon and the stars, which You have ordained; What is man that You take thought of him, And the son of man that You care for him? Yet You have made him a little lower than God, And You crown him with glory and majesty! You make him to rule over the works of Your hands; You have put all things under his feet, All sheep and oxen, And also the beasts of the field, The birds of the heavens and the fish of the sea, Whatever passes through the paths of the seas. O Lord, our Lord, How majestic is Your name in all the earth!

Prayer

O Lord, our Lord, how excellent is Your name in all the earth, who have set Your glory above the heavens!

Out of the mouth of babes and nursing infants You have ordained strength, because of Your enemies, that You may silence the enemy and the avenger. When I consider Your heavens, the work of Your fingers, the moon and the stars, which You have ordained, what is man that You are mindful of him, and the son of man that You visit him? For You have made him a little lower than the angels, and You have crowned him with glory and honour. You have made him to have dominion over the works of Your hands, and You have put all things under His feet. All sheep and oxen, even the beasts of the field, the birds of the air, and the fish of the sea, that pass through the path of the seas. Keep my eyes fixed on You. Keep my mind fixed on the things above. You have given me authority to trample over serpents and scorpions and over all the power of the enemy, but above all, You have blessed me, and permitted my name to be written in the Lamb's book of life. May I never cease to consider You, or to dwell on the work of Your hands. Keep me, Father, that I do not cease to be mindful of You, so that You are all I see, You are all I perceive, and You are all I permit. O Lord, our Lord, how excellent is Your name in all the earth!

In Jesus' name I pray, amen.

PSALM 9

Scripture

I will give thanks to the Lord with all my heart; I will tell of all Your wonders. I will be glad and exult in You; I will sing praise to Your name, O Most High. When my enemies turn back, They stumble and perish before You. For You have maintained my just cause; You have sat on the throne judging righteously. You have rebuked the nations, You have destroyed the wicked; You have blotted out their name forever and ever. The enemy has come to an end in perpetual ruins, And You have uprooted the cities; The very memory of them has perished. But the Lord abides forever; He has established His throne for judgment, And He will judge the world in righteousness; He will execute judgment for the peoples with equity. The Lord also will be a stronghold for the oppressed, A stronghold in times of trouble; And those who know Your name will put their trust in You, For You, O Lord, have not forsaken those who seek You. Sing praises to the Lord, who dwells in Zion; Declare among the peoples His deeds. For He who requires blood remembers them; He does not forget the cry of the afflicted. Be gracious to me, O Lord; See my affliction from those who hate me, You who lift me up from the gates of death, That I may tell of all Your praises, That in the gates of the daughter of Zion I may rejoice in Your salvation. The nations have sunk down in the pit which they have made; In the net which they hid, their own foot has been caught. The Lord has made Himself known; He has executed judgment. In the work of his own hands the wicked is snared. Higgaion Selah. The wicked will return to Sheol, Even all the nations who forget God. For the needy will not always be forgotten, Nor the hope of the afflicted perish forever. Arise, O Lord, do not let man prevail; Let the nations be judged before You. Put them in fear, O Lord; Let the nations know that they are but men. Selah.

Prayer

Father God,

I will praise You, O Lord, with my whole heart. I will tell of all Your marvellous works, that those I tell will hear it, and their hearts and minds will receive You. I will be glad and rejoice in You. I will sing praise to Your name, O Most High. Make me glad in You. Make me rejoice in You always, no matter my season of life, my Father God. Nothing unholy can enter Your presence, so I thank You that through the death of Your Son Jesus I am now under the Blood, and in Your sight I am perceived as holy. Redeem my mind and my flesh, that I may think and conduct myself from the holy position for which You have positioned me. The enemy makes attempts at destruction as if they are final, but You, O Lord, endure forever. You have authority over all things. You are the King of kings and the Lord of lords. You are a refuge for the oppressed, a refuge in times of trouble. And those who know Your name will put their trust in You, for You, Lord, have not forsaken those who seek You. I am not satisfied with how much I know You, Lord. I want to know more. Show me more of You, and do not allow me to be a hindrance to knowing You deeper. I will sing praises to You, Lord, and declare Your deeds among the people, for You are worthy of it all. Thank You that You do not forget the cry of the humble. Thank You for having mercy on me, O Lord. You see me. You consider the trouble I face from those with selfish motives. You have delivered me from death by the power of Your death and resurrection, Lord Jesus. You have taken on the death meant for me and exchanged it for Your eternal life. Give me boldness to testify to all You have done. You work all things for good because of my love for You. Make sure I never forget You, God, or what You have done. Put the fear of the Lord into me and cause it to take root in my heart, and strengthen. Do not let me be deceived by myself or any other, but let me only work in the wisdom and truth of You and Your love.

In Jesus' name I pray, amen.

Like a child sleeps under the watchful eye of a parent, so I will sleep under Yours

The Father & and His child

The Lord is my Father. His love is without conditions; I cannot work for it. I was born, loved by Him. He looks upon me as His precious child, for that's what I am in His eyes. He is the good Father, the Father that every man should look to as the standard of fatherhood. His eyes are on me, and they do not waver. Whether He is comforting me or He is correcting me, it is always done in love, and there is always love in His eyes when He looks at me. There is a desperation in the Father's heart to see His children saved. *Mimic me*, says the Lord. *Do what I do. Think as I think. Speak as I speak. Love as I love.* I will rest under His eyes, because if my Father is my watchman, who can harm me? He sits by my bed; He does not move. He watches, He waits, He covers, until my sleep ends and I awake, and even then still, He watches, He covers, He waits. I run to my Father day and night, for like a child, I am always excited to see my Dad, no matter how long or how little time has passed between our time together.

PSALM 10

Scripture

Why do You stand afar off, O Lord? Why do You hide Yourself in times of trouble? In pride the wicked hotly pursue the afflicted; Let them be caught in the plots which they have devised. For the wicked boasts of his heart's desire, And the greedy man curses and spurns the Lord. The wicked, in the haughtiness of his countenance, does not seek Him. All his thoughts are, "There is no God." His ways prosper at all times; Your judgments are on high, out of his sight; As for all his adversaries, he snorts at them. He says to himself, "I will not be moved; Throughout all generations I will not be in adversity." His mouth is full of curses and deceit and oppression; Under his tongue is mischief and wickedness. He sits in the lurking places of the villages; In the hiding places he kills the innocent; His eyes stealthily watch for the unfortunate. He lurks in a hiding place as a lion in his lair; He lurks to catch the afflicted; He catches the afflicted when he draws him into his net. He crouches, he bows down, And the unfortunate fall by his mighty ones. He says to himself, "God has forgotten; He has hidden His face; He will never see it." Arise, O Lord; O God, lift up Your hand. Do not forget the afflicted. Why has the wicked spurned

> God? He has said to himself, "You will not require it." You have seen it, for You have beheld mischief and vexation to take it into Your hand. The unfortunate commits himself to You; You have been the helper of the orphan. Break the arm of the wicked and the evildoer, Seek out his wickedness until You find none. The Lord is King forever and ever; Nations have perished from His land. O Lord, You have heard the desire of the humble; You will strengthen their heart, You will incline Your ear To vindicate the orphan and the oppressed, So that man who is of the earth will no longer cause terror.

Prayer

Father God,

Why does it feel at times as though You are far away? As if You hide when trouble arises, allowing wickedness to have its way? Father God, help me to see correctly, and perceive You rightly. For the wicked in his pride persecutes the poor, and I do not understand where You are. The wicked boasts of his heart's desire, and I do not understand why he is not silenced. The wicked blesses the greedy and renounces the Lord, and I do not understand how he gets away with it. You are in none of the wicked man's thoughts, Lord, and his countenance is proud. Why does it seem as though despite his wickedness, the wicked man prospers in all his ways? How is it that his heart is not convicted, and You are out of his sight? I do not understand it, Lord. But I pray You would reach even this kind of wicked man where they are at and cause them to turn from their wicked ways. Turn their hearts of stone to hearts of flesh, and humble they who are stuck in their pride. Convict their hearts of wickedness, and do not stop until there is no wickedness left. Let them not say, "I shall never be moved; I shall never be in adversity". And, Lord, if I have been this wicked person, and these ways have been my own, and the heart's desire of this wicked has been my heart, restore me. If I have had a mouth full of cursing and deceit and oppression, or trouble and iniquity have been under my tongue, touch my tongue and cleanse me in Your refining fire. Protect the innocent from the wicked who lurk in the shadows, or lie in wait to catch the poor. Protect the helpless and the fatherless, for You do justice to the fatherless and the oppressed, that the man of the earth may oppress no more. Let no man justify themselves, saying in their hearts, "God has forgotten; He hides His face; He will never see". I thank You that You do not forget the humble. You are the helper of the fatherless. Restore the evil man, and bless me with Your discernment to perceive the evil in another and be able to pray for them with words of knowledge regarding them. The Lord is King forever and ever. The nations have perished out of His land. Lord, You have heard the desire of the humble; You will prepare their heart; You will cause Your ear to hear. Thank You for inclining Your ear to me.

In Jesus' name I pray, amen.

PSALM 11

Scripture

In the Lord I take refuge; How can you say to my soul, "Flee as a bird to your mountain; For, behold, the wicked bend the bow, They make ready their arrow upon the string To shoot in darkness at the upright in heart. If the foundations are destroyed, What can the righteous do?" The Lord is in His holy temple; the Lord's throne is in heaven; His eyes behold, His eyelids test the sons of men. The Lord tests the righteous and the wicked, And the one who loves violence His soul hates. Upon the wicked He will rain snares; Fire and brimstone and burning wind will be the portion of their cup. For the Lord is righteous, He loves righteousness; The upright will behold His face.

Prayer

Father God,

Help me to keep my trust in You in all things, and if I ever question in my heart Your faithfulness, remind me You are here, present and intentional. When the wicked make efforts of evil against me, let me not look to myself, and what I can do in my own strength, but to You. Let me not view them through my eyes, but through Yours. For You have made me a holy temple for Your Spirit to dwell in, and have given me authority to be a vessel that Your kingdom may pour out onto the earth. Use me in the midst of evil, that You may be glorified. Your throne is in heaven, Your eyes behold all, and You test the righteous. So test me, Lord, and make me come out of Your testing strengthened in faith, firm in foundation, steadfast in prayer, persistent in worship, devoted to You. You have freed me, that the portion of my cup is everlasting life with You. Thank You. You are righteous, Lord, and You love righteousness. Behold me, and transform me from glory to glory as I behold You.

In Jesus' name I pray, amen.

PSALM 12

Scripture

Help, Lord, for the godly man ceases to be, For the faithful disappear from among the sons of men. They speak falsehood to one another; With flattering lips and with a double heart they speak. May the Lord cut off all flattering lips, The tongue that speaks great things; Who have said, "With our tongue we will prevail; Our lips are our own; who is Lord over us?" "Because of the devastation of the afflicted, because of the groaning of the needy, Now I will arise," says the Lord; "I will set him in the safety for which he longs." The words of the Lord are pure words; As silver tried in a furnace on the earth, refined seven times. You, O Lord, will keep them; You will preserve him from this generation forever. The wicked strut about on every side When vileness is exalted among the sons of men.

Prayer

Father God,

Do not allow me to put an end to my faithfulness. Convict me so that my yes is yes, and my no is no, and my faith is shown by my works. Help me to discern the person who speaks idly, with flattering lips and a double heart when they speak. Convict me and keep my heart humble, so that I am never comfortable being a person like this, so that my tongue does not speak proud things, or my lips give false flatteries. Thank You for rising up against the oppression of the poor and the sighing of the needy, and for setting them in the safety which they yearn for. Your words are pure words, Lord, like silver tried in a furnace of earth, purified seven times. Keep me, O Lord, and preserve me from this generation forever. Though the wicked prowl on every side when vileness is exalted among men, I shall not fear, for You are with me, and Your mercy endures forever.

In Jesus' name I pray, amen.

"I heard you."

The God who sees & the broken.

I heard you, my child. I heard the way your voice broke, and came out as a whimper against your tears and clenched throat. Do not think I ignored you. It broke My heart to hear your pain. Please understand I am doing something; you may not understand right now, but you don't have to understand to trust me. You don't have to know My plan to be comforted by My power and authority and control. Stay mine; I will never let you go. Feel Me holding you. Tighten your arms around Me, and dig your face into My chest. You can cry on Me. I will fix it. I will help. I will make it all go away. Just don't let go, do you hear Me? Don't let go of Me.

PSALM 13

Scripture

How long, O Lord? Will You forget me forever? How long will You hide Your face from me? How long shall I take counsel in my soul, Having sorrow in my heart all the day? How long will my enemy be exalted over me? Consider and answer me, O Lord my God; Enlighten my eyes, or I will sleep the sleep of death, And my enemy will say, "I have overcome him," And my adversaries will rejoice when I am shaken. But I have trusted in Your lovingkindness; My heart shall rejoice in Your salvation. I will sing to the Lord, Because He has dealt bountifully with me.

Prayer

Father God,

When I feel like You have forgotten me, and when I question how long You will hide Your face from me, help me to perceive You, and discern what You are doing in that moment. When I am consumed by the counsel of my own soul, when my mind ruminates obsessively, and I see no clarity, no hope, no understanding, to the point where I feel the oppression of the enemy as if he has the victory, remind me of my authority in You. Transform me by the renewing of my mind. Restore my thoughts, Father God. Fix my eyes on You, on what You say, not on what I say, or what the enemy says. Cast out the lies, and replace them with Your truths. Fortify my faith and strengthen the power of Your grace at work within me, that I may live as Your child. I know You hear me, O God, and I thank You that I can come boldly to Your throne of grace. Enlighten my eyes. Reveal Yourself to me. I want to see You. I will praise Your name, and I will glorify Your name, for greater is He who is in me, than he who is in the world, and that my soul knows very well. But search me, Father God, search me, Lord, if my soul does not know the power of Your name, or the absoluteness of Your authority, and rectify my understanding. Purify me, Father. Heal me. I trust in Your mercy, and I rejoice in Your salvation. Make my heart pure, my understanding deep, that I may worship You and praise Your name in spirit and in truth. I will sing to You, Lord, for You have dealt bountifully with me.

In Jesus' name I pray, amen.

PSALM 14

Scripture

The fool has said in his heart, "There is no God." They are corrupt, they have committed abominable deeds; There is no one who does good. The Lord has looked down from heaven upon the sons of men To see if there are any who understand, Who seek after God. They have all turned aside, together they have become corrupt; There is no one who does good, not even one. Do all the workers of wickedness not know, Who eat up my people as they eat bread, And do not call upon the Lord? There they are in great dread, For God is with the righteous generation. You would put to shame the counsel of the afflicted, But the Lord is his refuge. Oh, that the salvation of Israel would come out of Zion! When the Lord restores His captive people, Jacob will rejoice, Israel will be glad.

Prayer

Father God,

I pray that when You look down from heaven upon the children of men to see if there are any who understand, who seek God, that You would see me and I would be acceptable and pleasing in Your sight. Do not let those who say 'there is no God' prosper in his ways, but turn their hearts of stone to hearts of flesh. Reveal Yourself to them as Creator, Father, Saviour, Helper, the God who sees. Give knowledge to the workers of iniquity, that they may become aware of You, that You are true and good and righteous, and aware of themselves, that they may repent and seek You with a contrite heart. I thank You that You, Lord, are our refuge, and even those who were once contributors to the perverse generation can come to You and find refuge and have their wickedness exchanged for Your righteousness. I will rejoice and be glad in You, Father God, Lord of all, righteous and mighty.

In Jesus' name I pray, amen.

PSALM 15

Scripture

> O Lord, who may abide in Your tent? Who may dwell on Your holy hill? He who walks with integrity, and works righteousness, And speaks truth in his heart. He does not slander with his tongue, Nor does evil to his neighbor, Nor takes up a reproach against his friend; In whose eyes a reprobate is despised, But who honors those who fear the Lord; He swears to his own hurt and does not change; He does not put out his money at interest, Nor does he take a bribe against the innocent. He who does these things will never be shaken.

Prayer

Father God,

I thank You that You have made me a dwelling place for Your Holy Spirit. You have made me a tabernacle where You may abide because of Your work on the cross. You have made me righteous in Your sight. Help me to walk in righteousness, Father. Make me walk in the spirit, and not in the flesh, that my conduct may testify of the position of my spirit, which has been restored by Your blood. May the meditation of my heart and the words of my mouth be pleasing in Your sight, Lord Jesus. Let only truth take root in my heart, and anything that is not of truth, uproot it and cast it out, Lord God. Thank You, Father God. Thank You. May my conduct be a witness to those still living in the flesh, to those still abiding in wickedness, who do not honour You. You make me immoveable by Your blood, for You have said I will not be moved. Strengthen my fear for You, Lord, that I may honour You, and in wisdom I may behave and respond to all things in a way that is righteous and pleasing in Your sight.

In Jesus' name I pray, amen.

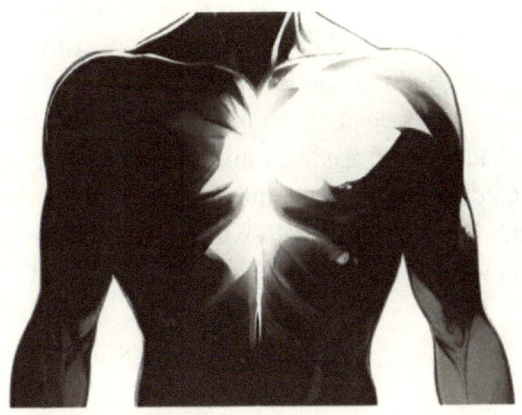

Sanctify Your servant, that Your grace may abound over my flesh.

The God of grace & the flesh

The grace of God is the power He imparts to us to overcome our flesh. The grace of God instructs us to deny ungodliness, and be holy as He is holy. We are called to live righteously, doing all things unto the Lord; not from our own strength, but His. My flesh is my enemy. It does not desire that I live in a manner pleasing to God, with reverence and understanding and wisdom. My flesh would rather indulge, and why shouldn't it? It has only this physical life to live, it does not pass into eternal life with me. Therefore, my flesh does not care where my spirit goes for the rest of its life. My flesh is bitter, telling my spirit, *'you get the rest of eternity but I only have now, so I will do what I want, and I'll be damned if you try to stop me'*. So the flesh wars with the spirit, to take dominion over my life. I need His Spirit, His grace, to win this war. My flesh is like a spoiled brat who expects submission. But I have been saved by the Lord Jesus Christ, and I am no longer a slave to my flesh, but to God. Does that stop my flesh from trying to take back what it once had? Never. And so I must be intentional to submit under God all that I say, all that I think, all that I desire, all that I do. For it is not up to us whether we will serve or not, but who we will serve.

PSALM 16

Scripture

Preserve me, O God, for I take refuge in You. I said to the Lord, "You are my Lord; I have no good besides You." As for the saints who are in the earth, They are the majestic ones in whom is all my delight. The sorrows of those who have bartered for another god will be multiplied; I shall not pour out their drink offerings of blood, Nor will I take their names upon my lips. The Lord is the portion of my inheritance and my cup; You support my lot. The lines have fallen to me in pleasant places; Indeed, my heritage is beautiful to me. I will bless the Lord who has counseled me; Indeed, my mind instructs me in the night. I have set the Lord continually before me; Because He is at my right hand, I will not be shaken. Therefore my heart is glad and my glory rejoices; My flesh also will dwell securely. For You will not abandon my soul to Sheol; Nor will You allow Your Holy One to undergo decay. You will make known to me the path of life; In Your presence is fullness of joy; In Your right hand there are pleasures forever.

F. C. Villani

Prayer

Father God,

Preserve me, for in You I put my trust. You are my Lord, my goodness is nothing apart from You, and if I have all things but not love then I have nothing. Make me delight in Your saints, in Your Spirit moving through Your people. Those who idolise and worship another God only sow destruction for themselves, Father. Fix their eyes on You, Father, and make sure my conduct can testify that You are the one true living God, glorified and greatly to be praised. I will not be tolerant of their sin, but I will love them as You love them, and I will choose to respond to them out of Your heart, not my own. Keep me in this, Lord, and establish me, that I may hold myself to my words to You. Convict me when I am not meeting Your standard, that I may never become complacent or lukewarm, that I may not be spat out of Your mouth. O Lord, You are the portion of my inheritance and my cup; You maintain my lot, what You have given me. You have blessed me Lord with a good inheritance. Continue to bless me with Your counsel, Lord, and mould my heart to always be able to receive it, in whichever way it comes to me. Do not let my heart give false instruction, but let it always be surrendered to Your instruction, Father God. Thank You, Father, that because You are for me, I shall not be moved. I ask You to go before me, Lord. Be my lead, my protection, my direction. Make my heart glad in You. You have paved a way, that my soul does not have to be subject to the enemy, Father God, and does not need to follow the world. Strengthen me that I may live as Your child. Show me the path of life, Lord, and keep me in Your presence, for in it is the fullness of joy. Make me desire Your presence with hunger and thirst, that I may be satisfied by You forever.

In Jesus' name I pray, amen.

PSALM 17

Scripture

Hear a just cause, O Lord, give heed to my cry; Give ear to my prayer, which is not from deceitful lips. Let my judgment come forth from Your presence; Let Your eyes look with equity. You have tried my heart; You have visited me by night; You have tested me and You find nothing; I have purposed that my mouth will not transgress. As for the deeds of men, by the word of Your lips I have kept from the paths of the violent. My steps have held fast to Your paths. My feet have not slipped. I have called upon You, for You will answer me, O God; Incline Your ear to me, hear my speech. Wondrously show Your lovingkindness, O Savior of those who take refuge at Your right hand From those who rise up against them. Keep me as the apple of the eye; Hide me in the shadow of Your wings From the wicked who despoil me, My deadly enemies who surround me. They have closed their unfeeling heart, With their mouth they speak proudly. They have now surrounded us in our steps; They set their eyes to cast us down to the ground. He is like a lion that is eager to tear, And as a young lion lurking in hiding places. Arise, O Lord, confront him, bring him low; Deliver my soul from the wicked with Your sword,

> From men with Your hand, O Lord, From men of the world, whose portion is in this life, And whose belly You fill with Your treasure; They are satisfied with children, And leave their abundance to their babes. As for me, I shall behold Your face in righteousness; I will be satisfied with Your likeness when I awake.

Prayer

Father God,

I perceive within myself that my prayer to You right now is not being spoken from deceitful lips, but if it is, and You have seen or perceived what I have not, correct me and purify my tongue. If You see uprightness in me Lord, bless me. Test my heart and see if You can find anything in it, for it is my intention that my mouth should speak holy words, true words. Keep me off the paths of the destroyer, Lord, and uphold my steps in Your paths, that my footsteps may not slip. I call upon You in this moment, Lord, for You are the God who sees, for You are the God who hears. Show Your marvellous lovingkindness by Your righteous right hand and save me from those who rise up against me. Keep me as the apple of Your eye; hide me under the shadow of Your wings from the wicked who oppress me, from my deadly enemies who surround me. Open their hearts, Lord, that they may no longer speak proudly with their mouths. Arise, O Lord, confront my enemies and cast them down, and remind me of my authority in You, that I may not lay hold of what You have already put away. Satisfy me in You, Lord. Show me Your face in righteousness, for I will be satisfied when I awake in Your likeness, when You bring me from glory to glory as I behold You.

In Jesus' name I pray, amen.

PSALM 18

Scripture

I love You, O Lord, my strength. The Lord is my rock and my fortress and my deliverer, My God, my rock, in whom I take refuge; My shield and the horn of my salvation, my stronghold. I call upon the Lord, who is worthy to be praised, And I am saved from my enemies. The cords of death encompassed me, And the torrents of ungodliness terrified me. The cords of Sheol surrounded me; The snares of death confronted me. In my distress I called upon the Lord, And cried to my God for help; He heard my voice out of His temple, And my cry for help before Him came into His ears. Then the earth shook and quaked; And the foundations of the mountains were trembling And were shaken, because He was angry. Smoke went up out of His nostrils, And fire from His mouth devoured; Coals were kindled by it. He bowed the heavens also, and came down With thick darkness under His feet. He rode upon a cherub and flew; And He sped upon the wings of the wind. He made darkness His hiding place, His canopy around Him, Darkness of waters, thick clouds of the skies. From the brightness before Him passed His thick clouds, Hailstones and coals of fire. The Lord also thundered in the heavens, And the Most High uttered His voice, Hailstones and coals of fire. He sent out His arrows, and scattered them, And lightning flashes in abundance, and routed them. Then the channels of water appeared, And the foundations of the world were laid bare At Your rebuke, O Lord, At the blast of the breath of Your nostrils. He sent from on high, He took me; He drew me out of many waters. He delivered me from my strong enemy, And from those who hated me, for they were too mighty for me. They confronted me in the day of my calamity, But the Lord was my stay. He brought me forth also into a broad place; He rescued me, because He delighted in me. The Lord has rewarded me according to my righteousness; According to the cleanness of my hands He has recompensed me. For I have kept the ways of the Lord, And have not wickedly departed from my God. For all His ordinances were before me, And I did not put away His statutes from me. I was also blameless with Him, And I kept myself from my iniquity. Therefore the Lord has recompensed me according to my righteousness, According to the cleanness of my hands in His eyes. With the kind You show Yourself kind; With the blameless You show Yourself blameless; With the pure You show Yourself pure, And with the crooked You show Yourself astute. For You save an afflicted people, But haughty eyes You abase. For You light my lamp; The Lord my God illumines my darkness. For by You I can run upon a troop; And by my God I can leap over a wall. As for God, His way is blameless; The word of the Lord is tried; He is a shield to all who take refuge in Him. For who is God, but the Lord? And who is a rock, except our God, The God who girds me with strength And makes my way blameless? He makes my feet like hinds' feet, And sets me upon my high places. He trains my hands for battle, So that my arms can bend a bow of bronze. You have also given me the shield of Your salvation, And Your right hand upholds me; And Your gentleness makes me great. You enlarge my steps under me, And my feet have not slipped. I pursued my enemies and overtook them, And I did not turn back until they were consumed. I shattered them, so that they were not able to rise; They fell under my feet. For You have girded me with strength for battle; You have subdued under me those who rose up against me. You have also made my enemies turn their backs to me, And I destroyed those who hated me. They cried for help, but there was none to save, Even to the Lord, but He did not answer them. Then I beat them fine as the dust before the wind; I emptied them out as the mire of the streets. You have delivered me from the contentions of the people; You have placed me as head of the nations; A people whom I have not known serve me. As soon as they hear, they obey me; Foreigners submit to me. Foreigners fade away, And come trembling out of their fortresses. The Lord lives, and blessed be my rock; And exalted be the God of my salvation, The

> God who executes vengeance for me, And subdues peoples under me. He delivers me from my enemies; Surely You lift me above those who rise up against me; You rescue me from the violent man. Therefore I will give thanks to You among the nations, O Lord, And I will sing praises to Your name. He gives great deliverance to His king, And shows lovingkindness to His anointed, To David and his descendants forever.

Prayer

Father God,

Increase my love for You, O Lord, for You are my strength. You deliver me from the hands of the enemy. O Lord, You are my rock and my fortress and my deliverer. You are my God, my strength, and in You alone I will trust. You are my shield and the horn of my salvation, my stronghold. I call upon You, Lord, because You are worthy of my praise, for You save me from my enemies, and Your heart is pure. If I am ever surrounded by the pangs of death, or I am afraid of the floods of ungodliness, even then be my comfort and my salvation, Lord. Even then hear my cry and come to me, in my place of sorrow and fear, and deliver me. You are my protector. Who am I that Your anger is aroused for my sake? Who am I that You should come down into this place of darkness and vanquish my enemies? How great is Your love for me that You desire my deliverance? Who am I that You would bow the heavens and come to my aid? O worthy is Your name, Lord, greatly to be praised. You send from above, and You take me, and draw me out of many waters. You take me and lead me beside still waters. My salvation from Your work on the cross has delivered me from my greatest enemy, from he who hates me, who once in my ignorance I believed was too strong for me. You have been my support, and You have delivered me. I pray that You will delight in me. Have Your reward in me, Jesus. Bless me according to my righteousness, Lord, according to the cleanness of my hands. Purify me, and mould me as my Potter, that I may be like clay, pulled and stretched and shaped in Your hands. Blessed are the merciful, for they shall obtain mercy. Blessed are the pure in heart, for they shall see God. Blessed are the meek, for they shall inherit the earth. Make me merciful, make me pure in heart, and make me meek Lord. You are my Light; You cause my darkness to brighten. I can do all things through Christ who strengthens me. With God, all things are possible. Your way is perfect, Lord; Your word is proven and does not return void. You are the only effective shield to those who trust in You. For who are You, but the Lord? And who is a rock, except You? You have blessed my hands, You have blessed my mind, You have blessed my heart. You have blessed me to overcome my enemies. You have blessed me, that I may be a light for You, a light and witness that even strangers perceive in me, but it is all You. It is You they perceive, Your Holy Spirit, Your kingdom, Your light, Your heaven, and I am merely Your vessel. Make me like pure gold, transparent, that all may see You and know You through me, Lord. Thank You for considering me. Thank You for Your faithfulness. Bless Your Holy name through me.

In Jesus' name I pray, amen.

"Why do you resist Me?"

The Good Shepherd & the stubborn sheep

You don't see where you are going. Come off this path. Let Me lead you. There is nothing down here but pain and destruction, nothing but jealousy and false wisdom, nothing but impurity and selfish intentions. I am not down there. You have already tasted what life can be like without Me in it. Why don't you turn around? Your mind considers My words, but your feet carry you still down the place you should not go. Take control of your feet. Return with Me. You enter boldly into the arms of evil, of the one who hates you and wants to stop all goodness from coming to you, but I have given you My Spirit, that you may come boldly to My throne of grace. How much longer will you embrace the enemy and reject Me?

F. C. Villani

PSALM 19

Scripture

The heavens are telling of the glory of God; And their expanse is declaring the work of His hands. Day to day pours forth speech, And night to night reveals knowledge. There is no speech, nor are there words; Their voice is not heard. Their line has gone out through all the earth, And their utterances to the end of the world. In them He has placed a tent for the sun, Which is as a bridegroom coming out of his chamber; It rejoices as a strong man to run his course. Its rising is from one end of the heavens, And its circuit to the other end of them; And there is nothing hidden from its heat. The law of the Lord is perfect, restoring the soul; The testimony of the Lord is sure, making wise the simple. The precepts of the Lord are right, rejoicing the heart; The commandment of the Lord is pure, enlightening the eyes. The fear of the Lord is clean, enduring forever; The judgments of the Lord are true; they are righteous altogether. They are more desirable than gold, yes, than much fine gold; Sweeter also than honey and the drippings of the honeycomb. Moreover, by them Your servant is warned; In keeping them there is great reward. Who can discern his errors? Acquit me of hidden faults. Also keep back Your servant from presumptuous

> sins; Let them not rule over me; Then I will be blameless, And I shall be acquitted of great transgression. Let the words of my mouth and the meditation of my heart Be acceptable in Your sight, O Lord, my rock and my Redeemer.

Prayer

Father God,

Reveal Yourself to me in the handiwork of Your creation. Make me see how marvellous Your works are, that my soul may know it very well. Teach me the wisdom found in Your creation, Lord, and open my eyes to receive it. Make me understand the perfection in Your sacrifice, Lord, and to believe in its ability to convert the soul. Show me the certainty of Your testimony and its ability to make wise the simple. Make my heart rejoice in Your statutes, Lord, and the purity of Your commandments to enlighten my eyes. Make me fear You, Lord, for the fear of the Lord is clean and endures forever. Your judgements are true and righteous altogether, Lord. Make me desire them beyond the riches of this world, and to count them as sweeter than honey and the honeycomb. Your rod and Your staff are my comfort, Lord; Your convictions are a comfort to me. Warn me by Your commandments, and help me to keep them. Search me, Lord, purify me, and bring to my awareness my errors that I may discern them and understand them. Cleanse me from secret faults. I am Your servant, and just like You did not come to be served but to serve, I will serve You. Keep me from presumptuous sins, and let them not have dominion over me. Take pride from my heart and replace it with humility. Do not allow wickedness to find rest in me Lord. Let the words of my mouth and the meditation of my heart be acceptable in Your sight, O Lord, my strength and my Redeemer.

In Jesus' name I pray, amen.

PSALM 20

Scripture

May the Lord answer you in the day of trouble! May the name of the God of Jacob set you securely on high! May He send you help from the sanctuary And support you from Zion! May He remember all your meal offerings And find your burnt offering acceptable! Selah. May He grant you your heart's desire And fulfill all your counsel! We will sing for joy over your victory, And in the name of our God we will set up our banners. May the Lord fulfill all your petitions. Now I know that the Lord saves His anointed; He will answer him from His holy heaven With the saving strength of His right hand. Some boast in chariots and some in horses, But we will boast in the name of the Lord, our God. They have bowed down and fallen, But we have risen and stood upright. Save, O Lord; May the King answer us in the day we call.

Prayer

Father God,

Remind my heart and press an urgency on me to always seek You in the days which I am troubled. Defend me, Father. Send Your help to me, and strengthen me,, Lord. You desire mercy more than sacrifice. Teach me what this means to You, Lord, and how I can be pleasing in Your sight. My living sacrifice is a reasonable service to You, so I give this as an offering to You with a cheerful heart. And if my heart is not cheerful to do so, then make it so, Father God. Grant me according to my heart's desire, Lord, and fulfil Your purpose in me. Make my heart gladly rejoice in Your salvation, Lord. Be glorified and magnified in me, Lord, that my heart and my mind and my tongue and my life and my conduct may be as a banner declaring the name of the Lord. Receive my petitions with Your grace and love, and respond to them according to Your will. Anoint me with Your holy oil, that I may pour oil at Your feet and return it to You. May my oil be a pleasing offering, and may my life be a sweet fragrance lifted to Your nostrils. Have Your reward in me, Lord Jesus Christ. Some trust in chariots, some in horses, and some trust in the works of their hands, but I will remember the name of the Lord. Never let me forget Your name, Lord, or take it in vain. Have mercy and grace upon me, Father, that when my eyes have fallen off You, and I have forgotten Your name, You will remind me, You will align my vision, and posture my thoughts and heart to You. Bless Your holy name, Lord.

In Jesus' name I pray, amen.

PSALM 21

Scripture

O Lord, in Your strength the king will be glad, And in Your salvation how greatly he will rejoice! You have given him his heart's desire, And You have not withheld the request of his lips. Selah. For You meet him with the blessings of good things; You set a crown of fine gold on his head. He asked life of You, You gave it to him, Length of days forever and ever. His glory is great through Your salvation, Splendor and majesty You place upon him. For You make him most blessed forever; You make him joyful with gladness in Your presence. For the king trusts in the Lord, And through the lovingkindness of the Most High he will not be shaken. Your hand will find out all your enemies; Your right hand will find out those who hate you. You will make them as a fiery oven in the time of your anger; The Lord will swallow them up in His wrath, And fire will devour them. Their offspring You will destroy from the earth, And their descendants from among the sons of men. Though they intended evil against You And devised a plot, They will not succeed. For You will make them turn their back; You will aim with Your bowstrings at their faces. Be exalted, O Lord, in Your strength; We will sing and praise Your power.

Prayer

Father God,

Thank You for adopting me into Your royal family. As King, You have blessed me with a royal inheritance that I could not have gained on my own. It is only by grace through faith that I can walk in the authority of my King. You have redeemed my name. You have restored me. My identity is in You. You have given me life and life abundantly. You have clothed me with robes, You have put a ring on my finger, and You have rejoiced in my return. You have embraced me, even when anyone else would turn me away. I am blessed to have You, and I am blessed to know You. You are my blessing. I was lost, but now I am found. I was blind, and now I see. I was proud, but You have blessed me in my repentance and put a contrite spirit in me. Where I would have been content to merely serve in Your house, You have made me Your child, adopted, wanted, bought, loved. Be exalted, O Lord, in Your own strength. Make me delight in singing praises to You of Your power, Lord, that You may be delighted.

In Jesus' name I pray, amen.

Father, convict my heart, that my oil may never run dry.

The Bridegroom & the virgin

It is my responsibility to keep my lamp filled with oil. Each one's oil is their own. I cannot borrow another's, nor can I purchase it. But I can store up my own supply by maintaining my relationship with the Lord. Time with the Lord creates oil, and oil keeps the fire burning in my heart, and if the fire is always lit, I will walk in the spirit. Fuelled by a constant stream of oil, the fire will burn within me, purifying me like refined gold. The fire of God will burn, making me a light unto others, revealing God in my conduct and countenance, that He may be glorified. I do not want to die without oil. And I do not want to live without fire.

PSALM 22

Scripture

My God, my God, why have You forsaken me? Far from my deliverance are the words of my groaning. O my God, I cry by day, but You do not answer; And by night, but I have no rest. Yet You are holy, O You who are enthroned upon the praises of Israel. In You our fathers trusted; They trusted and You delivered them. To You they cried out and were delivered; In You they trusted and were not disappointed. But I am a worm and not a man, A reproach of men and despised by the people. All who see me sneer at me; They separate with the lip, they wag the head, saying, "Commit yourself to the Lord; let Him deliver him; Let Him rescue him, because He delights in him." Yet You are He who brought me forth from the womb; You made me trust when upon my mother's breasts. Upon You I was cast from birth; You have been my God from my mother's womb. Be not far from me, for trouble is near; For there is none to help. Many bulls have surrounded me; Strong bulls of Bashan have encircled me. They open wide their mouth at me, As a ravening and a roaring lion. I am poured out like water, And all my bones are out of joint; My heart is like wax; It is melted within me. My strength is dried up like a potsherd, And my tongue cleaves to my jaws; And You lay me in the dust of death. For dogs have surrounded me; A band of evildoers has encompassed me; They pierced my hands and my feet. I can count all my bones. They look, they stare at me; They divide my garments among them, And for my clothing they cast lots. But You, O Lord, be not far off; O You my help, hasten to my assistance. Deliver my soul from the sword, My only life from the power of the dog. Save me from the lion's mouth; From the horns of the wild oxen You answer me. I will tell of Your name to my brethren; In the midst of the assembly I will praise You. You who fear the Lord, praise Him; All you descendants of Jacob, glorify Him, And stand in awe of Him, all you descendants of Israel. For He has not despised nor abhorred the affliction of the afflicted; Nor has He hidden His face from him; But when he cried to Him for help, He heard. From You comes my praise in the great assembly; I shall pay my vows before those who fear Him. The afflicted will eat and be satisfied; Those who seek Him will praise the Lord. Let your heart live forever! All the ends of the earth will remember and turn to the Lord, And all the families of the nations will worship before You. For the kingdom is the Lord's And He rules over the nations. All the prosperous of the earth will eat and worship, All those who go down to the dust will bow before Him, Even he who cannot keep his soul alive. Posterity will serve Him; It will be told of the Lord to the coming generation. They will come and will

> declare His righteousness To a people who will be born, that He has performed it.

Prayer

Father God,

When it feels like You have forsaken me, remind me that You have promised to never leave me nor forsake me. Remind me of Your faithfulness. Give me grace that I may be able to discern You in this moment. When You feel far away, encourage me to seek You even more fervently. Help me to perceive the seasons You have me in, and show me why there is a season for everything and a time for every purpose under heaven. Keep my heart on You, that when I cry out it is always to You, that when I need help I turn to You and Your ways, knowing in my heart that I am going to the right One. Even when it hurts, Lord, remind me to praise You in that moment. Mould my heart so even when I am hurting and scared I can declare Your goodness. Be enthroned upon my praises, Lord, and fill me with the fullness of Your joy. Pull me from darkness, and transform me by the renewing of my mind, so I do not compare myself with my brothers and sisters in Christ, that I do not see the way You have heard them and delivered them and look back at myself and wonder why my deliverance has not come. I don't want to view myself as a worm. I want to think the thoughts You have for me. I want to see myself through Your eyes. I want to know You deeply so when the end of my trouble has not yet come I can think of You and know it will not last, that You will deliver me, and You have delivered me before. When I feel empty, when I feel out of place and insecure, when my heart melts down from my chest into my stomach, embrace me. I need to feel You in that moment. I need to see You in that moment. Hold me, and show me Your face. Take the tension from my shoulders, and separate the clenching of my jaws. Though I am weak, You are strong; You are my strength and my Redeemer. Fix my eyes on You, that I may praise You and glorify Your name. I want to be able to praise You and stir up faith even in my struggle, even in my pain, even when I am emotionally exhausted, for even then should You be glorified. You are worthy. You are righteous. You deserve all the glory.

In Jesus' name I pray, amen.

PSALM 23

Scripture

> The Lord is my shepherd, I shall not want. He makes me lie down in green pastures; He leads me beside quiet waters. He restores my soul; He guides me in the paths of righteousness For His name's sake. Even though I walk through the valley of the shadow of death, I fear no evil, for You are with me; Your rod and Your staff, they comfort me. You prepare a table before me in the presence of my enemies; You have anointed my head with oil; My cup overflows. Surely goodness and lovingkindness will follow me all the days of my life, And I will dwell in the house of the Lord forever.

Prayer

Father God,

You, Lord, are my shepherd; I shall not want. What can I want? For You sustain me. You make me to lie down in green pastures. You lead me beside the still waters. You restore my soul. You lead me in the paths of righteousness for Your name's sake. Even if I walk through the valley of the shadow of death, through evil and temptation, I will fear no evil, for You are with me. Your rod and Your staff, they comfort me. I thank You Father God, for You prepare a table before me in the presence of my enemies. You anoint my head with oil; my cup runs over. Cause my cup to overflow, Lord, and cause me to bless You by pouring Your oil upon Your feet. Surely goodness and mercy shall follow me all the days of my life, and because of You, I dwell in the house of the Lord forever.

In Jesus' name I pray, amen.

PSALM 24

Scripture

The earth is the Lord's, and all it contains, The world, and those who dwell in it. For He has founded it upon the seas And established it upon the rivers. Who may ascend into the hill of the Lord? And who may stand in His holy place? He who has clean hands and a pure heart, Who has not lifted up his soul to falsehood And has not sworn deceitfully. He shall receive a blessing from the Lord And righteousness from the God of his salvation. This is the generation of those who seek Him, Who seek Your face—even Jacob. Selah. Lift up your heads, O gates, And be lifted up, O ancient doors, That the King of glory may come in! Who is the King of glory? The Lord strong and mighty, The Lord mighty in battle. Lift up your heads, O gates, And lift them up, O ancient doors, That the King of glory may come in! Who is this King of glory? The Lord of hosts, He is the King of glory. Selah.

Prayer

Father God,

Increase my understanding of Your greatness. Increase my awe of You, Lord. Give me revelation and wisdom of Your magnitude and Your majesty, Father God. Reveal Your nature to me. Make me know You as God, the Creator, Who established the heavens and the earth, Who founded the earth with wisdom. Clean my hands and purify my heart. Forgive me if I have lifted up any idols above You, and give me discernment to perceive the areas of my life where I have done this. Bless me with Your wisdom that I may steward Your forgiveness. Convict my heart that my 'yes' may be 'yes' and my 'no', 'no', Lord. You are the King of glory. You are strong and mighty; You are mighty in battle. You are the overcomer, the victorious, and You have made the enemy Your footstool. Thank You that in You I have victory over my enemies. Let me not get in the way of bringing heaven on earth, especially in the face of my enemies.

In Jesus' name I pray, amen.

Fortify my faith, Lord, that it may be impenetrable.

The Refuge & the weak in faith

My faith cannot be an effective shield if it is hanging by a thread. I must be persuaded by the reality of the gospel. Convince me, Father. Persuade me of Your truth, for if my faith is not as a fortress, it can be overrun, brought to its knees in surrender to doubts and confusions and lies. How can I strengthen my faith? How can it be fortified? How can I be convinced of His word? I must be in it; I must be in His word, for faith comes by hearing, and hearing by the word of God. I need the word of God to hear Him, to stir up my faith. In His word His truth will be revealed, and in this my faith will increase. Truth is like bricks, layered atop each other and glued together with the cement of the Holy Spirit to build a wall of faith. This is my shield.

PSALM 25

Scripture

To You, O Lord, I lift up my soul. O my God, in You I trust, Do not let me be ashamed; Do not let my enemies exult over me. Indeed, none of those who wait for You will be ashamed; Those who deal treacherously without cause will be ashamed. Make me know Your ways, O Lord; Teach me Your paths. Lead me in Your truth and teach me, For You are the God of my salvation; For You I wait all the day. Remember, O Lord, Your compassion and Your lovingkindnesses, For they have been from of old. Do not remember the sins of my youth or my transgressions; According to Your lovingkindness remember me, For Your goodness' sake, O Lord. Good and upright is the Lord; Therefore He instructs sinners in the way. He leads the humble in justice, And He teaches the humble His way. All the paths of the Lord are lovingkindness and truth To those who keep His covenant and His testimonies. For Your name's sake, O Lord, Pardon my iniquity, for it is great. Who is the man who fears the Lord? He will instruct him in the way he should choose. His soul will abide in prosperity, And his descendants will inherit the land. The secret of the Lord is for those who fear Him, And He will make them know His covenant. My eyes are continually toward the Lord, For He will pluck my feet out of the net. Turn to me and be gracious to me, For I am lonely and afflicted. The troubles of my heart are enlarged; Bring me out of my distresses. Look upon my affliction and my trouble, And forgive all my sins. Look upon my enemies, for they are many, And they hate me with violent hatred. Guard my soul and deliver me; Do not let me be ashamed, for I take refuge in You. Let integrity and uprightness preserve me, For I wait for You. Redeem Israel, O God, Out of all his troubles.

Prayer

Father God,

To You I lift up my soul and deliver my heart. I trust in You, my God, and I thank You that I can come boldly to Your throne of grace. I thank You that, despite me, You have seated me in heavenly places, and guide me to pray from my seat and not from my fleeting place here on earth. Do not let me grow tolerant in laying hold of the enemy and his attempts to steal, kill, and destroy all You have for me. Let me not grow complacent in assisting the enemy in destroying me and interrupting Your will for me. Show me Your ways, O Lord. Teach me Your paths. Lead me in Your truth and teach me, for You are the

God of my salvation. On You I will wait all the days of my life, for where else can I go to receive the words of eternal life? Those who wait on You will renew their strength. Strengthen me, Lord. Fortify my faith. Give me Your faith. Heaven's faith. Unwavering. Childlike. Fervent. I thank You that Your mercies are new every day, that Your character is one of gentleness and lovingkindness. You are the God who was and is and is to come. You are the same yesterday, today, and tomorrow. I thank You that You cast my sins far from Your memory, that You blot out my filth and when You see me, You see Your Son. The precious blood of Your Son Jesus covers me; it drapes me like skin and coats me like a garment. You are good and upright, my Lord. Make me humble, and in my humility teach me Your way, and guide me in justice. Help me to keep my covenant with You, to walk in the spirit and not in the flesh, to give You my reasonable service with a grateful heart and to pour my oil upon Your feet. May my oil be a sweet fragrance to You. Have Your reward in me, Abba. Increase my fear and reverence for You, Father God, and place peace in my heart for the choices of Your teaching. Make me to dwell in prosperity. Make me meek, for the meek will inherit the earth. Share Your secrets with me, Father; entrust me with Your mysteries. Come down upon me, Holy Spirit, as an all-consuming fire, and as a dove, resting upon me all of my days. Keep my eyes on You, that I may not stumble to the left or to the right, no matter the storm or battle surrounding me.

Keep my eyes on You, even when my enemies are numerous, for Your name is the name above every name, and it causes every knee to bow and demons to cower and convulse and beg for mercy. Thank You for going before me, for delivering me from my distresses, and carrying me through all of my afflictions. Keep my soul in Your presence, keep my heart in Your presence, keep my tongue in Your presence, keep my flesh in Your presence. Let integrity and uprightness preserve me, for I wait for You, Lord. Open the eyes of my heart, and give me eyes to see and ears to hear, that I may recognise Your voice and heed it quickly, for You are my Good Shepherd, and I am Your sheep. Do not let me be scattered.

In Jesus' name I pray, amen.

PSALM 26

Scripture

Vindicate me, O Lord, for I have walked in my integrity, And I have trusted in the Lord without wavering. Examine me, O Lord, and try me; Test my mind and my heart. For Your lovingkindness is before my eyes, And I have walked in Your truth. I do not sit with deceitful men, Nor will I go with pretenders. I hate the assembly of evildoers, And I will not sit with the wicked. I shall wash my hands in innocence, And I will go about Your altar, O Lord, That I may proclaim with the voice of thanksgiving And declare all Your wonders. O Lord, I love the habitation of Your house And the place where Your glory dwells. Do not take my soul away along with sinners, Nor my life with men of bloodshed, In whose hands is a wicked scheme, And whose right hand is full of bribes. But as for me, I shall walk in my integrity; Redeem me, and be gracious to me. My foot stands on a level place; In the congregations I shall bless the Lord.

Prayer

Father God,

Consecrate me for Your satisfaction. Be pleased by my heart. Sanctify it. Cleanse it. Purify it. Examine me, my God, and prove me. Try my mind and my heart. I ask You to mould me. I am Your willing clay, and You are my potter. With Your hands, fashion my heart to Your likeness. Break my heart for what breaks Yours. Create in me a heart of integrity and intolerance. Make me intolerant to evil, intolerant to wickedness, intolerant to idolatry, and intolerant to hypocrisy, whether that be me in myself or in others. Help me to love despite my intolerance, Lord, knowing that love does not equal tolerance, nor does it rejoice in inquity, but it rejoices with the truth. Help me to discern myself and those I come across righteously, that I may not account them for their sin or identify them by their sin, but as the lost sheep for which You search for, the prodigal son You wait upon, and run toward once he has returned. Keep me clean and focused in the assembly of the wicked, that I may hold steadfast to You, Father God, and my conduct may give witness to them of Your glory and truth, that they may see You, Father God. Make my voice the voice of thanksgiving, that I may tell of all Your wondrous works, Lord, and others may hear of them and encounter You in their hearts. Make me a habitation, a place where Your glory dwells. Permit me to be a Bethany for You, my

Lord, a place where You may rest all the days of my life. Redeem me and make me merciful, Lord, for the merciful shall obtain mercy. Replace the portions of wickedness and foolishness in my heart with the clay of integrity. Search me and expose my heart, and if You find double-mindedness, pluck it out. Consecrate me to You, Father God, that I may worship You in spirit and in truth, and bless You among people with pureness of heart and humility.

In Jesus' name I pray, amen.

PSALM 27

Scripture

The Lord is my light and my salvation; Whom shall I fear? The Lord is the defense of my life; Whom shall I dread? When evildoers came upon me to devour my flesh, My adversaries and my enemies, they stumbled and fell. Though a host encamp against me, My heart will not fear; Though war arise against me, In spite of this I shall be confident. One thing I have asked from the Lord, that I shall seek: That I may dwell in the house of the Lord all the days of my life, To behold the beauty of the Lord And to meditate in His temple. For in the day of trouble He will conceal me in His tabernacle; In the secret place of His tent He will hide me; He will lift me up on a rock. And now my head will be lifted up above my enemies around me, And I will offer in His tent sacrifices with shouts of joy; I will sing, yes, I will sing praises to the Lord. Hear, O Lord, when I cry with my voice, And be gracious to me and answer me. When You said, "Seek My face," my heart said to You, "Your face, O Lord, I shall seek." Do not hide Your face from me, Do not turn Your servant away in anger; You have been my help; Do not abandon me nor forsake me, O God of my salvation! For my father and my mother have forsaken me, But the Lord will take me up.

> Teach me Your way, O Lord, And lead me in a level path Because of my foes. Do not deliver me over to the desire of my adversaries, For false witnesses have risen against me, And such as breathe out violence. I would have despaired unless I had believed that I would see the goodness of the Lord In the land of the living. Wait for the Lord; Be strong and let your heart take courage; Yes, wait for the Lord.

Prayer

Father God,

You are my light and my salvation, whom shall I fear? You are the strength of my life; of whom shall I be afraid? When the enemy has risen up against me, Your blood has interceded. They stumble and fall at the victory of Calvary. Mighty is my King, and that my soul knows very well. Though the enemy encamps around me, ready and waiting to cause me to slip, my heart shall not fear. And though the enemy wars in the spiritual realm, I am confident in the Lord of hosts, my Commander of the victorious armies of heaven. I will gird myself with the whole armour of God, putting on the helmet of salvation, strapping on the breastplate of righteousness, tightening the belt of truth around my waist, and equipping my arm with the shield of faith. The gospel of peace I will put on my feet, and the sword of the Spirit, which is Your word, I will wield in my hand. I am a soldier in Your army, O Lord of hosts. I will trust in You forever. My every fear must surrender. Make this my one desire, O Lord, that I may dwell in Your house all of my days, to behold Your beauty and to inquire of You as Your temple. You have made me a temple, a dwelling place for Your Holy Spirit. Overcome me now, Lord, for I am not satisfied. Fill up Your servant, Your temple, so that the doors and walls of this temple cannot contain the overflow of Your Spirit. You have set me upon a rock, upon a firm foundation. You have set me on a mountain to be a light to the world. You have made me as the salt of the earth, that all peoples may thirst for You and Your righteousness. There is no longer a tabernacle to offer sacrifices of joy, for I am Your tabernacle, Lord. Therefore I will make sacrifices in my conduct, in my reasonable service, that You may find joy in me. And I will sing to You, Lord; I will sing praises to Your blessed name. I pray that the song in my heart remains as this, "Your face, Lord, I will seek". You are the God who sees. For in my darkness, You saw me. In my agony, You saw me. When I cried, You collected my tears, knowing one day You would restore my joy and not a single tear would be wasted. You have never departed from me, but I have departed from You. In my heart and in my mind, in my conduct and in my tongue, I have departed from You. Forgive me, Father, for You deserve so much more than the rags I have given You. But I thank You that You are faithful, and Your love endures and abounds forever. You are merciful to me, Father God. Who am I that I may receive favour in Your sight? Who am I that You would be faithful to me? You have been my help. You have cared for me. Restore me, that I may never depart from You in word or thought or desire. Deliver me when my own foolishness causes the enemy to be like a vulture, ravaging my heart. Do not allow me to lose heart, knowing the goodness and mercy of God follow me all the days of my life. And help me to be of good courage as I wait on You, for in my waiting, You strengthen my heart, and in my waiting, my faith is fortified.

In Jesus' name I pray, amen.

I will guard my heart with righteousness.

The Righteous & His breastplate.

Righteousness is the standard of what is pleasing in the eyes of God and what is not. Righteousness will cover my heart and penetrate it the way the blood of Christ pours out and coats my spirit, ensuring nothing is seen but Himself. Coat me, Righteousness, like a cloak preventing rain from touching the body. Impurity will not touch my heart. And if unrighteousness is found in my heart, then the power of God will suck it out like a vacuum, collecting the dirt that shouldn't be there. Righteousness is as a breastplate, protecting the vital organs that are necessary for life. Abundant life requires a righteous heart.

PSALM 28

Scripture

To You, O Lord, I call; My rock, do not be deaf to me, For if You are silent to me, I will become like those who go down to the pit. Hear the voice of my supplications when I cry to You for help, When I lift up my hands toward Your holy sanctuary. Do not drag me away with the wicked And with those who work iniquity, Who speak peace with their neighbors, While evil is in their hearts. Requite them according to their work and according to the evil of their practices; Requite them according to the deeds of their hands; Repay them their recompense. Because they do not regard the works of the Lord Nor the deeds of His hands, He will tear them down and not build them up. Blessed be the Lord, Because He has heard the voice of my supplication. The Lord is my strength and my shield; My heart trusts in Him, and I am helped; Therefore my heart exults, And with my song I shall thank Him. The Lord is their strength, And He is a saving defense to His anointed. Save Your people and bless Your inheritance; Be their shepherd also, and carry them forever.

Prayer

Father God,

To You I give my cry, for You are my Rock. Blessed are those who mourn, for they will be comforted. Be clear and direct in Your comfort toward me, Father God. I do not want silence from You; I want to feel the embrace of Your presence. I want to perceive Your eyes and Your smile upon me. If it pleases You, grant me the desire of my heart, for without You I will fall deeper into my pain. I cannot take it, Lord. Despite my cries, I will lift my hands in worship, Lord, for even in pain You are my Deliverer, and even in my sadness You are my Healer. You are my strength and my shield. My heart trusts in You safely, and I am helped. Make my heart glad to rejoice in You, God, for You have brought me to Yourself and delivered me from wickedness and sanctify me from my flesh. You are the saving refuge of Your anointed. Bless Your inheritance and have Your reward in me. You are my Shepherd, Lord, and I shall not want beyond You. Bear me in Your arms. Hold me. Keep me. I am Yours.

In Jesus' name I pray, amen.

PSALM 29

Scripture

Ascribe to the Lord, O sons of the mighty, Ascribe to the Lord glory and strength. Ascribe to the Lord the glory due to His name; Worship the Lord in holy array. The voice of the Lord is upon the waters; The God of glory thunders, The Lord is over many waters. The voice of the Lord is powerful, The voice of the Lord is majestic. The voice of the Lord breaks the cedars; Yes, the Lord breaks in pieces the cedars of Lebanon. He makes Lebanon skip like a calf, And Sirion like a young wild ox. The voice of the Lord hews out flames of fire. The voice of the Lord shakes the wilderness; The Lord shakes the wilderness of Kadesh. The voice of the Lord makes the deer to calve And strips the forests bare; And in His temple everything says, "Glory!" The Lord sat as King at the flood; Yes, the Lord sits as King forever. The Lord will give strength to His people; The Lord will bless His people with peace.

Prayer

Father God,

Show me the value of You, that I may honour You with glory and strength. Help me to conduct myself in the beauty of holiness, that my worship may be pure and pleasing in Your sight. I incline my ear to You, Lord, and pray that You would enable me to hear Your voice that hovers over the waters, to perceive Your glory. I want to know You as the God whose voice is powerful, the God whose voice is full of majesty. I want to understand You, to understand the perspective of Your voice being able to break and splinter the cedar trees of Lebanon. Make me understand the knowledge of Your voice, Father God, Abba, that it is a voice that divides flames of fire, and shakes the wilderness, the voice that makes the deer give birth and strips the forests bare. Cause me to shout of Your glory, Father God, to proclaim the glory of the Lord. Entrust me with an understanding heart, Lord, that I may stand in awe at Your wonder and not count Your nature as mediocre or timid. For You are enthroned before Your creation, and You sit as King forever. Bless me with strength, Lord, and bless me with Your peace that surpasses all understanding.

In Jesus' name I pray, amen.

PSALM 30

Scripture

I will extol You, O Lord, for You have lifted me up, And have not let my enemies rejoice over me. O Lord my God, I cried to You for help, and You healed me. O Lord, You have brought up my soul from Sheol; You have kept me alive, that I would not go down to the pit. Sing praise to the Lord, you His godly ones, And give thanks to His holy name. For His anger is but for a moment, His favor is for a lifetime; Weeping may last for the night, But a shout of joy comes in the morning. Now as for me, I said in my prosperity, "I will never be moved." O Lord, by Your favor You have made my mountain to stand strong; You hid Your face, I was dismayed. To You, O Lord, I called, And to the Lord I made supplication: "What profit is there in my blood, if I go down to the pit? Will the dust praise You? Will it declare Your faithfulness? "Hear, O Lord, and be gracious to me; O Lord, be my helper." You have turned for me my mourning into dancing; You have loosed my sackcloth and girded me with gladness, That my soul may sing praise to You and not be silent. O Lord my God, I will give thanks to You forever.

F. C. Villani

Prayer

Father God,

Stir delight and gratitude in me, that I may extol You with pure praise and pure joy, for You have delivered me again and again and placed my enemies beneath my heel. You heard me, Lord, when I cried out to You for help, and You healed my brokenness. I am still being perfected, and I am still being sanctified for Your name's sake; therefore, God, I ask that You reveal to me the areas of my heart and my mind that You want to heal and restore, correct and purify. Make me a person of holiness. You have saved me from the pit of hell by Your salvation, but it is not just from death that You have kept me alive. You have birthed me again with new life, and have blessed me that I may not only have life with You eternally, but life here abundantly. Let me never forget this truth, Lord. Remind me constantly of the blessings only found in You, that I may desire to sing praises to You and give thanks to Your holy name without ceasing. You have every right to be angry with me, and yet Your forgiveness and Your love and favour has been my testimony. You have been faithful when I have not. And when I have wept through the night, You have caused a shout of joy to rise from my heart to my lips in the morning. You have not left me in the night; You have not left me in my weeping. When I have mourned, You have comforted me. When I am hunched forward by the ache in my chest, You have flooded me. You have overcome me. And even when You have not done so immediately, the time You allow it has drawn me to You. It has refined me. And it has caused me to seek Your face with desperation. I would rather be desperate for You than live as if I can do this alone, with a false joy and a false peace that comes with the absence of trouble. For when I have been secure and stable, when I have sat in the blessing and answered prayer, I have said with pride and ignorance in my heart "I shall never be moved", but if I can't see Your face, there is no security, there is no stability, there is no blessing, there is no peace. So never turn Your face from me, Lord, and do not allow me to turn my face from You. I welcome Your correction. I welcome Your staff. I welcome Your rod. Do not let me stray, nor let me wander off. And if I do, find me. Follow me. Take me in Your arms and return me to the flock, Lord. For You are my Good Shepherd, and I am Your sheep. You bind up my brokenness, and strengthen what is sick and weak within me. You feed me in good pasture and make me to lie down well fed. You turn my mourning into dancing, and when I have felt suffocated, You have loosened death's hold and girded me with gladness, that my soul may sing praise to You and not be silent. O Lord my God, give me a heart that desires to thank You forever.

In Jesus' name I pray, amen.

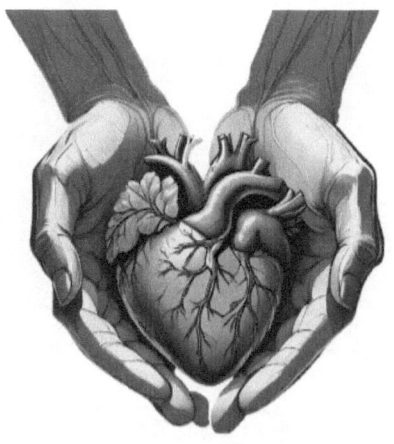

Take this heart, Lord, and return it, purified.

The Refiner & the heart

My heart is not my own, for it is no longer I who live, but Christ. My heart alone is rotten and dirty, and requires purification. If I allow Him, the Lord will purify this heart until it is transparent, a reflection of Himself. If I allow Him, His desires will be my desires. If I allow Him, His heart will be my heart. If I allow Him, I will see Him, for the pure in heart will see God. But it is then a choice, is it not? I must allow Him. It takes my surrender to allow the work of God to come to completion in my heart. I must surrender. *Nevertheless Lord, not my will, but Yours, be done.* Yes, Jesus. If the will of God was enough for You, it is enough for me. Not my will, but Yours, be done in me.

ABOUT THE AUTHOR

Francesca Villani, published as F. C. Villani, currently takes residence with her husband in Melbourne, Australia. Francesca actively pursues her dream and purpose of being a full-time author. She endeavours to nurture the world with truth, one story at a time. Francesca wholly believes that there is power in words, and such power should be used with the utmost care, for with your words you can either give life, or take it. Francesca strives to share her words in the hopes that in some way, they may give life to those reading them.

IG: @fcvillaniauthor

YouTube: The Reading Writer

www.fcvillaniauthor.com

ALSO BY F. C. VILLANI

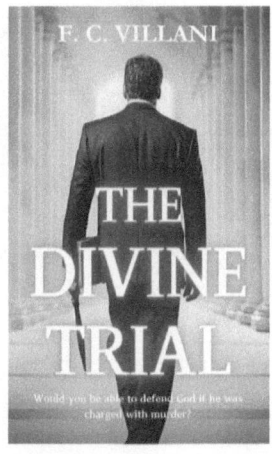

Isaac Stewart, criminal defence lawyer of Ox County, wakes up in his office one morning only to learn he has been requested to defend a man charged with being an accomplice to murder, by none other than the accused himself.

After their first meeting, Issac learns his client is not a man at all, but God in the flesh, and despite the doubts telling him he shouldn't, Issac agrees to defend him.

However, as information of the case begin to unfold, Issac learns his client is potentially responsible for the brutal murders of three women and their sons, and once he has reviewed the heinous details of their deaths, Issac is left with a question that threatens to dismantle everything he has ever believed: is God truly innocent?

www.ingramcontent.com/pod-product-compliance
Lightning Source LLC
Chambersburg PA
CBHW022017290426
44109CB00015B/1210